UNDER THE LEAF

A GARDEN OF POETRY

BY JOAN E. JANSSEN

Proceeds from this book of garden poems benefit
the Herb Society of America's gift to the country
The National Herb Garden
in the National Arboretum, Washington D.C.

UNDER THE LEAF

This little book was seeded by a group
of garden related poems written for the
SAGE LEAVES, the newsletter of the
Wisconsin Unit of the Herb Society of America.
It has been fun to compose thoughts into
rhymes and now to print them together,
as you have asked me to do.
Some poems, not about gardens, have been
added as I discovered them in the computer
while planning for this book.
I hoped my poems would make you smile.
Are you?

JOAN E. JANSSEN has been a member
of The Herb Society of America
for over 30 years. She has been Editor
of the SAGE LEAVES for the Wisconsin
Unit for many years. Her articles
and poetry have appeared in the
HERBARIST, the annual publication of
The Herb Society of America.
She was awarded the Certificate of Appreciation
in 1996 from The Herb Society of America.
Joan served as Chairman of the
Wisconsin Unit in 1978-80 and in 1996-98.
She lectures for garden groups to spread
the lore of herbs and enjoys visiting herb gardens
and meeting herb gardeners everywhere.

Grateful Acknowledgement is given to
Jean Fisher who acted as editor for these
poems.
Jean received the Certificate of Appreciation
Award of the Herb Society of America in 1992.
Jean has served as Chairman
and in other roles for the Wisconsin Unit.
Jean also has served as a member of the
Board of the Herb Society of America.

The design for the cover and the illustrations
decorating UNDER THE LEAF are the work of
Virginia Joan Janssen.
Virginia is a graduate of the University of
Colorado and of the School of Medallic Art of
the Italian Mint in Rome, Italy.
Virginia specializes in medallic sculpture and
produces other art objects.

CONTENTS

SUMMER INVITATION

Come walk with me in my garden
Just come and admire my flowers
For every weed I ask pardon
Keeping them out would take hours.
Step on the rosy pink bricks
Stroll mosaic pathways I've made
Sniff at a sun-dappled bloom
Do admire the work of my spade.
How I wish I had magical powers
That I could cast a secret spell
To create a quilt of soft colors
Where tiny fairies could dwell.
But see the butterfly rest on a flower
The bee and the hummingbird too
Perhaps they noticed your pleasure
They've come to visit with you.

I

BEWARE!

Did you know that every garden
                hides a den of hungry thieves?
Yes, they lurk among the berry vines
                they prowl on fresh green leaves.
Earwigs and thrips, white flies and slugs
                that gardeners deny are there
Hide below in the hot midday sun and
                munch in the evening air.
Organic beds are fun for them
                they slurp the plants to waste
Spray is their undoing
                they do abhor that taste.
They just adore a burger
                of compacted sticky loam
They wiggle footsy feelers
                and make themselves at home.

These pests welcome their friends
                into your tidy, weed-free rows
They dare you to end the spread
                of their 'sticky-fingered' toes
After evening mastication
                a whitish foam they spread
To let you gardeners know
                how they enjoyed their daily bread
Call a halt to this chomping life
                before only stems remain
Stop those thieves, those bugs and flies
                that are the gardener's pain.
Save the celosia, the mallow
                and the friendly marigold
Slather the spray, point the hose
                to stop these thieves so bold.

MOON GAMES

When the moon goes to bed
And lowers his golden head
He sweeps up the stars
Stores them in jars
The better to keep
The better to sleep.

QUEEN OF THE GARDEN

Regal and radiant, she strikes her pose
The Queen of the garden—the velvet red rose.
Slender of stem, brilliant of hue
Regal in bearing, she unfurls to our view.
Her wrap of soft petals, curled to beguile
Prickly thorn clasps enclose with style
Her sparkling crown glistens in morning dew
Over twisted curl clusters, wind laced anew.
What dreams does she offer or memories awake.
Her fragrance pervades the breath that we take
Her scent is her power—her legend profound
Her Majesty the Rose Queen holds us spellbound.

THOUGHTS AS WE WORK

Please, Master Gardener—
Search out that seed within our soul
                enliven it with the sunshine of your glory,
                enrich it with the splendor of your grace,
                endow it with the comfort of your love,
                educate it with the brightness of your might.
Nurture that seed that You gave us
with the care that only You can.
                Sow with abundant goodness
                Sprinkle with heavenly blessing
                Weed with patient firmness
                Gather with loving friendship.
We thank You for the privilege
of blooming in your garden.

DEAR FRIEND, DID YOU KNOW?

Friends are flowers that never fade
Friends are gifts that can't be repaid.
Friends take part when dreams are made
Friends hold fast where problems raid.
Friends clasp tight when you're afraid
Friends just know if you need their aid.
Friends laugh and love as life is played
Friends dare the loneliness to invade
Friends exchange smiles for errors you made
Friends brighten the day as love they trade

ARE YOU READY?

Springtime wants to come
Can you feel it in the lane?
Jump up and be ready
Birds will dance out in the rain.
Lavender clouds will drift over our heads
Roots and shoots wake from deep, murky beds.
Nature creates fashions in soft, silky greens
Woods and meadow become pastoral scenes.
Under toadstools, insects explore hi-tech wings
Grasshoppers practice favorites they will sing.
In just a few days, sunflowers will start
Sun will shine down to warm your heart
The softest of breezes will caress your cheeks
All part of springtime in the next few weeks.
Springtime is ready, just wait a bit more
Springtime is ready to knock at our door.

PETER RABBIT

Happy Birthday to the first herb lover I knew
Who tasted the garden greens as they grew
Who ate the parsley when it was free
And went to bed with chamomile tea.
Over 100 years his story's been told
Of Peter Rabbit who never grows old
His tales we heard in the nursery
They taught us to eat our broccoli
So gardeners everywhere pay heed
Eat those greens to be healthy indeed!

MOON MOVES

Man in the Moon, your pristine light
Bears witness to your power and might
You set the seasons and time the tide
By your transient travel our life we bide.
It is your wish, 0 spirit great
That sets our moods and makes our fate.
Mr. Moon, you are more than worldly light
You plan our nature through season's night.
Routinely the seeds await your cue
The structure of life depends on you.

ODE TO THE GARDENER

We wish you a restful season
We wish you some books a pleasin'
We wish you the peace of winter
That's our wish for you. Then...
We wish you a plannin' season
We wish catalogs a teasin'
We wish you a golden springtime
That's our wish for you.
May you enjoy the herbal kingdom
And use the outdoor freedom
We wish you a fruitful harvest
That's our wish for you.

A BOOK SHOP ROMANCE

A firefly and a bookworm met
On a star-crossed magic eve
In a special kind of book shop
In the treetops, would you believe?
The firefly glowed at the bookworm
And she demurely folded her wings
As the bookworm suggested espresso
To talk over books and things
The firefly, flattered and flustered
Beamed her antenna bright
To follow the gallant bookworm
In the door of the book world that night.

Into the book stacks she followed his lead
Too timid to explain that she couldn't read
That very night she began to piece out letters
Especially the word spelled L-O-V-E
At daybreak she took with her quite a few books
To read in her kingdom above.
This isn't the end of the love match
For she really did learn to spell
She read novels and cookbooks
And traveled in books, as well.
Quite often she met the bookworm
Who had opened the book store door
But her answer to him was sad, you see
Next to books, he was a bore.

NUTTY NOURISHED BUGS

Does the earwig need a barber shop
      to visit every week?
How does she keep her wavy wig
      looking at its peak?
When the thrip clan plans an outing
      to do the things they like
Why must they pick on leaves
      for their walking- tour or hike?
Do the tidy whiteflies use the cleaners
      to preserve their pristine duds?
Is that why they must fly around
      avoiding garden mud?
When they cluster in a cloud-site
      are they off to bed at night
Or moving to a meal-site
      where they chomp 'till day is light.
Flies like to chum around us
      as we picnic on the sand
Why can't these creatures understand
      we wish them back in buggy land.

THE GREEN THUMB TURNS BROWN

Now I put my plot to rest
Just as birds desert their nest
I clear spent stems and turn the soil
Loathe to end the season's toil.
But falling leaves in brown and red
Help craft a patch for winter's bed
Soon earth will slumber day and night
Beneath a quilt so snowy white.
Garden plans await a fresh spring start
But spend the winter blooming in my heart.

THE OTHER SIDE OF THE MOON

It's the same round moon that glowed in June
This moon inspired love words in many a tune
The same old orange, the same half-secret smile
The toothless pumpkin no longer can beguile.
It's afloat like a frigid ice-berg balloon
It's December now, it's not the June moon
Now an empty plate at the end of the day
Washed and dried to be put away.
The playful grin turns a smirking gleam, and
Radiates the brilliance of a cold cosmic beam.
In winter the milky way halo floats in high gear
So we can't read the chalkboard message sphere
Information lost until winter's end
Lost are the love words the moon tries to send.

PATIENCE

There's a long, long time till summer
Until then it's springtime we need.
There's a long, long time for waiting
Until it's time to plant the seed.
There is snow and ice a plenty
To freshen bulbs asleep below
Until the tulips and forget-me-knot
Rise up to say hello.
May the fairies of the garden
Dust color among the flowers
And bless them in their sleeping pods
To enhance their growing powers.
At last, we'll notice emerald shoots
Wholesome air will come our way
We gardeners must begin to work
Even though we call it play.

AS FALL APPROACHES

Good night dear garden, in your brown loamy bed
The curls have fallen from your leafy head
Your earth mom is calling it's time now to rest
Your animal friends do in their soft furry nest.
Good night, cicely and sorrel, thyme, bouncing bet
Sweet woodruff, oregano, sage, violet
I spread out the mulch quilt. I silently frown
Hope you're comfy in your leaf-lined gown.
Sweet dreams now, may snow blanket you
May you slumber till sunshine warms you through
As spring bulbs arise, may your new seed awake
I will be ready with trowel, trug and rake.

MOON'S PLAYTIME

Who makes the stars float in the sky?
Why are they placed up there so high?
 My little child, don't you know
The moon sends them in his handy rainbow.
He chooses each one from his quiver of love
And sends it to light up the sky above.
The moon loves all who watch below
He dazzles with his heavenly star show.
He comes out at night with his bow to play
He arranges his star toys to suit his own way.
He bids us "good eve" and points his star light
The moon is our friend all through the night.
When he has made funny faces shine his best
He drops behind the edge of the world to rest.
But the stars he has placed so high above
He leaves in place to remind of his love.

PLEASE, SPRING, COME AGAIN

Can we trust that spring will give birth
After cold fingers have grasped the earth
Will the sun release its frosty stare
Will soft rains make the bulbs aware
Will winter pass away with care
Will the ground be warm for the seeds
Will there be compost for their needs
Will tiny birds arrive from the skies
Will violets be teased enough to rise
Will snow and ice melt from sight
Will wind stop blowing with such might
Will new green shoots be pleased to appear
After that, we're sure, spring is near.

FRIEND RAIN

We like to say it's dancing
It resembles beads of pearl
We like to say its heavenly
Helps our coiffures curl
We say it's needed in the garden
Settles dust along the path
We say it's good for flowers
 Helps give the birds a bath
We pretend to miss the heavy clouds
That drift in from afar
We tell each other "rain is good
It washes off the car"
We pretend to like to hide inside
Don't mind canceled games
We announce we like rain's music
On our window panes.
Yet if caught out in a downpour
When our hair looks like a mop
We tend to tell the nasty truth
We wish this rain would stop!

IF YOU'RE A GARDENER

If in the passing of the seasons
You don't mind the winter's snow
If in the coat of white your garden wears
You can picture shoots below.
If you can browse the books of green
As you wait for the frost to melt;
If winter's just a passing scene
Whose fingers must be felt.
You're a gardener.

If as tulips and snowdrops peek a bit
And you can't wait to seed
If as longer days bring the world alight
You list tools and pots you'll need.
If the green house is a lingering spot
And you can hardly wait to start
If violets and snow drops make you smile
And flowers bloom in your heart.
You're a gardener.

If summertime is a gleeful chore
As your garden comes into its own
If you rest now a bit to appreciate
To admire the seeds you've sown.
If happiness grows within your breast
You'll know then you've met the test.
If you love to delight in your garden parade
If you also thank God for the earth She made
You're a gardener.

If fall has been a time for sighs
As plants are put to sleep
If tender herbs are sent indoors
With hopes to help them keep.
If weeding time is changed to walks
And hoes exchanged for rakes
If you hesitate to cover your plot
You've got the green thumb ache.
You're a gardener.

FRIENDSHIP

How warm to greet a friend
To glow in the light of their eyes
How comforting their clasp
How engaging their grasp
Even across many miles
Thoughts of a friend ring true
And bring a breath of freshness
Like a garden blessed with dew

CLOUD STYLE

As moon and sun meet
          to cast evening rays
They cast spells about to call
          clouds from their play
The cloud "kids" brush curls
          in lacy puffs on little heads
And in proper cloud fashion
          dress in layers for bed.
The layered look is in
          moonbeams like it, they say
That's why cloud-jammies
          are colored that way.
Clouds may wrap in beige and azure
          or vermilion or blue
Or almond or aqua
          or lavender-pink hue.
Sometimes clouds yawn in warm colors
          orange and red
They dress for sleep in comfort then
          not fashion instead.
Little cloud-layered "kids"
          sleep in mother nature's love
As the sky curtain closes
          the fashion show above.

LAVENDER LADY

A mysterious lady of every age
Whose fragrance wafts through history's page
Memories of old lace, dainty and sweet
Bouquets exude perfume exquisite to greet

A design copied for landscape display
The scent most desired even today
Simple gray spikes articulate grace
Aura evokes plans for tender embrace

Colored tints vary to violet, mauve or blue
 Paths and hedges drift to purple hue
An aromatic old world herb always the same
Legion are myths one delights to rename

The lavender fantasy travels worldwide
Intriguing secret lessons tucked inside
Culinary and medical values may yet be explored
The illusions and lore will forever be adored

NEVER A WEED

Which garden creed designates a weed
Of ambitious seeds that try hard to succeed.
Such flowers indeed are not really weed.
New England Asters spread out even faster
Indian grass shoots succeed from their roots
Thistle grows tall- heads above all
A proud purple brush alive without fuss
Queen Anne's powdered face lifts up with grace
Turning roadsides to lace in summer's embrace.
Chicory blue bears the weed label too
Her bright nodding head gardeners chop dead.
Hawkeye and golden rod decorate the sod
Milkweed and cat tail appear without fail.
Who dared to name these flowers the same
Who chose them a name lacking in fame
Fall's Necklace Beads all is the name to call.

THE COLD FACTS OF LIFE

I wonder why we live in this bleak, frigid air
When snow and cold winds make up daily fare?
Why should we shiver and cover our head
We could live in balmy warm states instead?
Perhaps it is because we like to wait
To watch sprouting trees growing hair
To enjoy the fresh breath we feel in the air.
For spring's glorious promise to prepare

VALENTINE

Of all ancient herbers known to exist
The name Valentine never was on the list
Now, this story I heard and it may be retold
Tells of a herber named Valentine in days of old.
He was a physician whose medicines one could savor
He combined bitter potions with honey to flavor
He cleansed with wine vinegar the wounds of the slain
And used freshly ground herbs to relieve the pain.
For his religion he was made a prisoner at last
He understood his ministry soon would be past.
But he sent a yellow crocus to a lass who was blind
Said he hoped for a miracle and signed Valentine.
"May this yellow crocus light your eyes from above
May your sight be restored through my message of love"
Perhaps his quaint story is a herbal message today
May the yellow crocus remind us of Valentine's way.

BOOKS, BOOKS, BOOKS

Why do you always want to read
What is this fuss about a book?
Whenever I need you I always know
You'll be reading in a quiet nook
Maybe you will learn the answers
Because you open a book to look
You may travel through history or space
You can learn to garden or cook
Without books the world would be empty
No help for those yearning to know
Without reading about our amazing world
Your life would be boring and slow

THE CHRISTMAS STORY ACCORDING TO JOAN

On a crisp, winter night God unfolded his plan.
He had worked on it since the world began.
It was the plan for His garden of charity and love
The plants were ready in the greenhouse above.
The earth would shelter a nursery room
Of souls who would strive to blossom and bloom.
In his plan, the maiden would conceive
On an earthly, frosty, clear blessed eve.
A babe would be born, His heavenly Son
To watch o'er His plants till the world was done.
He sent out angels to find a garden shed,
They selected a dark, shabby stable instead.
Then when they noticed where the animals fed
They filled it with straw to make comfy a bed.
So God's only Son whom He wanted to send
As the gardener of eternal man- plants to tend
Was born with horticultural work to do
To water and weed and harvest souls too.
For though God would plant each special seed
Some would be flowers, some would be weed.
This is my story of how God's garden grew
A story told in wonder each year anew.

SPRING FOR SURE

Surely spring is imminent
This has to be the time
When the lilac buds are peeking out
This is a certain sign.
It's time to hear the fairy folks
In plants along the walk
As they critique new flowers
And exchange fairy talk.
If you notice green dainty tips
In the plot along the wall.
Hang the pansy basket
Invite your friends to call.

HARVEST MOON

Shine on Harvest Moon, harbinger of fall
Shine your brilliant beacon on cornstalks tall.
In those straight rows searching crows glide
Behind quiet haystacks sleeping tractors hide.
Your ball of fire seems a huge firefly
Falling leaves shine as wind drifts them by
Stalks reach to your light to wither and dry
Frosty sparkles of dew gently waft from the sky.
You burnish the world with a beam so bright
Through the years, Harvest Moon, your gift of light
Paints beauty and peace in our universe at night.

SUMMER DILEMMA

In my garden looking at me
Herbs little faces make their plea
Ready for any recipe
Ready to flavor afternoon tea.
Rosemary is here, proud as can be
Basil shouts it's versatility
Chives remind me they are free
Parsley waves, hoping I'll see.
Thyme creeps over neath the willow tree
Silvery sage sits sunning near the peas.
Which should I choose for my herb recipe
Do you think that you and I would agree?

THE TEA PARTY

In a shady garden bower
At the best appointed hour
The lady bugs and spiders meet for tea.
There's a hustle and a bustle
Underneath a spreading flower
Because they chatter and they patter
Till the mealy bugs and earwigs seek to flee.
Sipping warm dew drops under leafy rooftops
They gossip to heart's desire
In their fancy winged attire.
They sup from bluebell cups
They lounge on daisy tufts
While they munch organic matter
From a tiny violet platter.
Eating bits of cookie crusties
Topped with toasted compost butter
A thousand wings aflutter
Help make music as they mutter
Sharing recipes for the batter
Of a cake to make them fatter

Yes, that would be a treat
For they simply love to eat
They discuss with buggy passion
Winged styles and gossamer fashion
Fox-gloves they rate but cat-tails they hate
The sound of garden chatter rises to high key
It's like the buzzing buzz of the honey bee
These tea parties in the spring
Have a happy, lilting ring
The reason for the celebration is quite clear
After winter slips away
They need to have their day
To wiggle out into the buggy land
And join into a buggy band
To play in garden soil and sand
And help give gardeners a hand.

GALAXY GARDEN

The old moon's grin hides behind icy cheeks
He doesn't smile in the winter weeks
But shows off his garden to our delight
Winter flowers that glow in the night.
He made his patterns in shapes and rows
In dippers and diamonds, whatever he chose.
He sprinkles all these with a luminous beam
He hoes and waters until they gleam.
Then lounges there on a cloud powder puff
Hiding his tools in a wispy lace muff
If he neglects filmy cloud fences to splice
His field produce drops as snow or ice
The old moon works hard at night up high
 He cares for his garden of stars in the sky.

EARTH DAY THOUGHTS

They tell us we should
        appreciate the worth—
To celebrate the special
        week of the Earth.
Let us try to imagine,
        if we can,
The value and weight
        of this gift to man.
The power of a forest,
        the bright summer morn,
Gentle stillness of winter,
        fall haystacks all shorn.
This can we measure—
        these gifts and their worth,
Not yearly, but daily—
        let's celebrate our earth!

THE LORD OF THE NIGHT

He reels in the day
                He holds power to delight
He is the night king
                The Lord of the Night.
His reign lasts just hours
                The world firm in his aim
Can't recover light
                Until day makes her claim.
The clouds must leap or curtsy
                To shield their weary ball
In the day's last hours
                As dark floats over all.
They may loathe
                to leave their playground,
To desert their earthly sphere
                yet they must
Stretch their pinky tutus
                They must follow without fear.
They frolic and they pout
                They dance and they sway,
They care they will be lost
                In the closing light of day

Those little clouds clutch together
                    They fluster and they fret
When the Lord of the Night
                    Surrounds them with his net
Stretching out their dusky fingers
                    In the colors they employ
They shrink away together
                    As he bids to end their joy.
It's dancing they crave
                    But at night they must rest,
Thus he swallows them all
                    In his ample weathered breast.

They long to keep together
                But are drawn to float afar
So behind them in the heavens
                They leave a little star.
The Lord pulls along that star
                As he begins to slip below
His wand waves away
                Those sleepy clouds aglow.
Behind him he trails
                A beribboned, spangled train
For only moon blush and
                Star dust elude his trailing rein.

When the Lord of the Night
          Meets the Queen of the Light
He offers to exchange
          Special keys to ignite
When he finds he can't replace
          That special needed key
He uses milky moonbeams
          To pay his transfer fee.
The Lord of the Night holds reign
          Through darkest hours
Until the sun and the moon
          Unleash their magic powers,
Promptly dawn and morning wed
          To set the world awake
They banish his kingdom's shadow
          For the fresh days sake.

TO ALL GARDENERS: GOOD WISHES!

Our wish for you as spring days arrive
Is finding all your plants alive
It's also compost worked in the soil
And rainy days to rest from toil.
If catalogs tease for just one plant more
We hope you can stop at three or four.
We wish that all your seeds will grow
Germinating on time in a nice straight row.
That blossoms bright burst forth in spring
That sun and rain will do their thing
That every seed sprouts from every pack
We wish you most a good strong back!

TREE TALK

Do not eavesdrop, mother said to me
But I can't avoid the chatter from a tree
The gnarled old oak will creak and groan
The supple locust gives only a moan
Dropping red and yellow leaflets from her grasp
The maple tree answers black crow's rasp
To punctuate, blue jay honks a sharp beep
Red squirrel scolds with ringing cheep
Pine trees do not wish to complain along
Their branches applaud in expressive song
High white pine stutters pierce the shade
So daisies dance in the sun dappled glade
The lacy twig patterns delight my eye
Trees gossip and wave as I pass by.

HISTORY OF LAVENDER

When Eve met Adam, the apple wasn't her charm
'Twas a bouquet of lavender she clasped in her arm
The rib he gave her may have been that scented twig
a lavender sprout that was just too big.

Cleopatra might have plotted with lavender steam
To coax Mark Anthony into her dream
It certainly led to circumstances unique
When Mark succumbed to her lavender mystique.

Victoria was known to use and adore
The study of lovely lavender love- lore.
We must wonder if Albert did enjoy
Lavender posies Vicki would employ?

When Emily Dickinson penned poetic words she chose
Sweet lavender scents from her note-paper arose
Bunches of lavender were arranged in her room
Her thoughts were the result of lavender bloom.

No doubt Zorro didn't recognize the fragrant scent
But Spanish lavender plants grew where he went.
His ardor increased as near lavender he came
He promised true love to each Spanish dame.

Betsy Ross probably made George wait at her door
While she spread lavender cuttings around on the floor.
He was her friend, but no chance did she take
Lavender fragrance helped her flag business make.

What do you think Molly Pitcher carried in that flask?
It was lavender water for a household task
She may have sniffed it as she straightened the sheet
Or tucked sprigs inside to mask hubby's feet.

The cherub of love, Cupid, needs lavender spray
To polish bow and arrow for Valentine's Day.
Lavender is a timeless, treasured scent
Year after year, "I love you" it meant.

ONCE IN A BLUE MOON

Once in a blue moon an unusual beam
Forces nature awake early from winter's dream.
Then grass carpets suck snow's blanket weave
Frost and ice heave, getting ready to leave;
Surprises press up from bulbs stored below
Primrose and snowdrops and violets show;
Tumbling creeks spill out winter debris
Trees empty branches come alive with glee;
Tiny eggs snuggle in fresh feathered nest,
Winds caress creatures awakened from rest;
Sun radiates warmth with satisfied mirth
Old Mother Earth will again give birth!

THE ATTIC

How can I let another purchase
These old and tired items
Too worn to be of value, because
They show marks of care and age.
My parents collected them
To make life easier and
To help brighten their way.
These possessions bear pride of ownership
Proof of their family love
Could I sell these faded photos?

These quaint carved frames, I remember?
They were fingered so fondly
By family and friends
Could I imagine such familiar portraits
In a faraway stranger's house?
Could these favorite frames surround
Another's smile or frown?
Let me hide them away like a treasure
And hold them for some later pleasure.

MY POETRY

I find it a pleasant pastime
In quiet evening hours
Finding rhymes in thoughts and ideas
For poems of herbs and flowers.
Outside my window I visualize the world
Images appear from far and near
Names and faces of herbs I know
Burst into rhythm happy and clear.
I plant a garden of leafy thoughts
These lines are like rows to me—
Each word is a seed in a plain white bed
The harvest is poetry for you and me

A TRAVEL PROBLEM

On the way to our garden, the springtime elf
Must have lost his way in spite of himself.
We wait for his paint brush to touch up our grass
To decorate our fields with his colorful mass
To coax the hyacinths and snowdrops to glow
To paint rosy morns and set showers to flow.

The springtime elf is due, why must we wait?
By March twenty-first we should celebrate.
Snowbanks are melting, one by one
Even the robins have seen fit to come.

Mischievous spring elf, with you we plead
Warm up the air, spread the sunshine we need.
We know you can travel, so why must we wait
Gardeners implore you to remember our date.

A LOVE STORY

A lady bug and an earthworm
                    dated one Solstice night
They met at an herb garden party
                    much to their delight
The lady bug admired the striped earthworm
While gently folding her wings,
The gallant worm made small talk chatter
About ph and garden things
The lady bug listened that starry eve
Thrilled by the worm she could hardly believe
My hero, she said, nodding her head
                    you're not only cute.
If you know all about compost,
                    you must be astute.
The next week he called to invite her down
Into his world beneath the earth's crown.
There, she made every effort
                    to help him sow seed
Although fearful of tangling
                    her wings in the weed
Among the damp rows she followed his lead
Too timid to mention sunlight was her need

At daybreak she flew to the sunflowers above
To decide if the worm and his work
                    she could love.
In gardens, she knew, love is easy to catch
Would this be the end of the wormy-bug match?
She returned to the worm's rows one dewy eve
And buried her head in her polka-dot sleeve.
She stammered the words in a ladylike rush
Accompanied by a most tender pink blush.
Said the lady bug shyly at the earthworm's door
You have taught me so very much garden lore
But I find dirty earth too much of a trial;
I can't live with you in a lowly ground aisle.

THE SCHOOL BUS

Spitting and splashing it stops at the gate
Red eyes flashing, it signals "wait!"
Grumbling and rumbling along the lane
Stopping and waiting amid sun and rain
It swallows up children to start the school day
For children must learn that life is not play.
But each trip aboard the bright yellow craft
Another step from home's trusty path
A step taken lightly never counting the cost
Not knowing each step is babyhood lost.
We know time must push their world to grow
They tell how they learn with papers to show.
It won't be the same child we put on their way
That bus changes each life every school day.
The large yellow transport is more than a bus
It is the first looming look away from us.

It picks up our children in the early morn
With bleeding red lights and a strident horn.
Does the driver on the bus think about this,
These jumps into the future does he miss
Does he know his bus means freedom,
            that he helps to chart the way
That his bus breaks mother's world apart
            as children start their day?
While mothers wave so bravely,
            and fuss over mittens and boots
They pat the heads of their little ones
            to remind them of their roots
The yellow bus opens life for each child in turn
Every tot must climb aboard ready to learn.

THE EVERLASTING GARDEN

A garden awoke calling shoots to stand tall
Teased by the warmth of an orange red ball.
Dew drops had dried at dawn's first kiss
The garden awoke in mystical bliss
The newest seedlings set in the row
Cried "what can we do, how shall we grow?"
So the greatest gardener opened up their pod
Straightened the stems and patted the sod
Beauty and love start thus from a seed
Tended by God as He sees the need.
He waters with goodness and helps it to flow
To creatures growing in weakness or woe.
Whose growth is enhanced by every good deed
Who flourish together, both plant and weed.

THE HONEY BEE

Apis mellifera is a most pompous title
For a soft and sticky insect who can't be idle.
Working around us he gathers liquid gold
To fill a waxy trademark amazing to behold.
It's hard to catch this creature free in daily flight
But no one knows if bees ever sleep at night.
Life is easy for this insect soft and fuzzy
Everyone is aware of his signature buzzy.
Floral scents attract him, this you will see
You don't want to meet him, accidentally.
Wearing prisoner stripes, and clear, filmy wing.
Bees answer back with their painful sting.
If one is spreading pollen, don't get in the way
If one comes in your path, run off, don't delay.

TULIPS, TULIPS, GOOD BYE

I think that I shall never see
A tulip nodding back at me.
A garden bed of waving faces
A handful placed in pretty vases
In spring I doubt if there will be
Bulbs I planted lovingly.
I'll search for sprouts so carefully
Did voracious beasties let them be?
Alas, I know the traveling deer
Come hungrily from far and near.
To reach my beds in time to eat
The tender, greenish leaf tips sweet.
In future springs I vow attack
To thwart the visiting white-tail pack
I'll turn to plants they shun to chew
The daffodils will have to do.

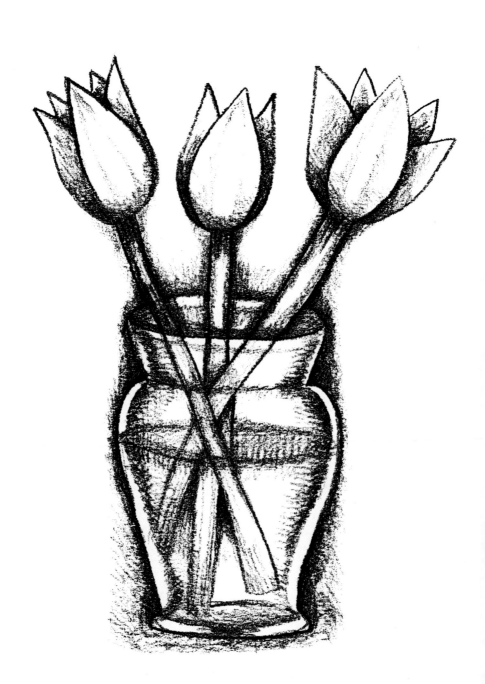

TRIBUTE TO SPICE

Spice is a happening, spice is hot
Spice is power, dull it's not
Spice means flavor, spice means taste
Shake it, sprinkle it or use it to baste.
Spice means zest, be sure to test
Spiced meals are a riot, why not try it?
Spice means seasoning come from afar
Spice is not just mustard in a jar
Spice is scent, spice is tang
Spice is aroma, meals with a bang.
Spice is sweet, it will perk up meat
Spice is hearty, spice makes a party
Spice adds color, spice adds crunch
Spice is a topping, a garnish to munch
Spice is a sophisticate, something with style
Shake it on top or dip into a pile
Spice is cumin, paprika, cayenne
Spice up today—if not today, when?

WHAT IS ENGLAND IS MADE OF?

black and white sheep, cattle asleep
ivy clad trees, wafting breeze
hay in sheaves, twining vines and leaves
boxy hedges, rocky ledges
open plains, sheltered lanes
a "ham" stone home, chalk furrows like foam
rooftops of thatch set in a garden patch
Queen Anne's lace raised, goldenrod praised
chimney pot tops and "comfort stops"
historic bridges, rocky 'tor' ridges
scented roses tempt our noses
holly hocks, neat rows of box
bracken ferns, flower filled urns
garden plans, tripod camera fans
backing up the bus, what a fuss,

a garden hostess with the mostest
houses of glass, hay wagons to pass
tree trunks of age, too huge to gauge
tiny window panes, restoration reigns
dove cotes and chicken pens,
                    peacocks and spotted hens
fountains and water 'rills',
                    window lace and curtain frills
burial mounds, hiking trails,
                    fire trucks and royal mails
Wilton and Stilton, carpets and cheese
gardeners and tradesmen happy to please—

THAT'S WHAT ENGLAND IS MADE OF!

GARDEN GUARDIAN

The garden gate in winter
                wears a wig of icicle curls
A dress of brown matted ivy
                and beads of sparkling snow pearls.
Her swinging arms now immobile
                impervious to wind's swift lash
Bound by left over spiral stems
                whipped into a sash.
Never seen to shiver
                locked in frost up to her knees
Leaves about her ankles
                swirl in piles and freeze.
Fingers undaunted by winter's frigid wrath
Silently keep pointing to the herb lined path.
Only moon light passes on crisp evening walks
By this graceful guardian of stiff, leafless stalks.
A metal sentinel offering an icy embrace
An out-of-work marker to the garden place.

SUBTLE SPRING

Be aware if you want to hear
Subtle suggestions that spring is near.
Spring is unruly, it sighs and it weeps,
Pushing wet, woolly clouds away as it sweeps.
Trees hold up naked black twigs needing sleeves
Waiting for nature's designer green leaves.
Golden haired willows kiss damp mossy ground
A fat belly robin yanks a worm he has found.
The fairies line-dance on toadstools at night
A frog band croaks tunes to their delight
Departing winds tease temperature to rise,
A lemon drop moon glows in soft, misty skies.
Pastel primrose spreads chartreuse fluffy arms
Bold tulip bows to bright daffodil's charms.
Sage, thyme and hyssop sprout shoots anew
Basil, rosemary, tarragon show a few, too.
Rain showers drops on scarecrow's hair
Subtle spring signs spring out everywhere.

THE DAY OF THE TULIP

Stretching luxuriously, I arise from my dream
Awakened along with friends budding green
Surrounded by warmed, sweet, brown earth.
On that important morning- the day of my birth.
My slender stem hides promise of baby bud
Gently twisting loose from a bulb held in mud.
Candy cane petal ends unfold in twisted curl
I watch my smart, stylish dress begin to unfurl.
Proud and aware like a Deb at the ball
With great grace I allow pointed leaves to fall
Everyone will glance at me in my row
I am perfect, I am lovely! this I do know.

Then! nearby, heavy footsteps, more than a few
I just might be trampled, what ever can I do?
If only I could sink and return to my place
If only I could hide in earth's soft embrace.
These are not footsteps of those who will view
but stamping deer who come to chew.
Where can I hide? I wave leaf arms about
I shudder- and wish for help I could shout
My stripes may attract them to come over here
Life will be short if they choose me, I fear.
I'm swallowed, it becomes quite damp and dark
My botanical ballet dance concludes in the park.

COMPLAINTS, COMPLAINTS

Plantain weed and chicory blue
What have I ever done to you?
Why do you loll in my garden space?
Flowers are crowded in that place.
Herbs would exist if your leaves didn't spread
No wonder I don't like your bold, curly head.
When I survey my patch, it's green I need
Not yellow clover or pink Joe pie weed.
Globe thistles will do, plain thistles aren't right
Old plain thistle just spreads with a might.
What was in that dirt I shoveled last fall
Does "blended soil" mean weeds and all
Well, all you weeds that love it here
Pack your up your roots and move to the rear.
Go out on the lawn or travel next door
I don't want you in my plot any more.

UNDER THE LEAF

Why are you surprised to find me here?
Under this leaf is my cozy abode
In summer I help in your garden plot
You see, I'm your garden toad.

This is my living room, and my muddy bed
In this kitchen, I dine in style.
Sometimes I must hurry to leave
When you scatter your compost pile.

Under the leaf in this jumble of weeds
Near the vegetable garden post
I catch millions of winged creatures
To change into yummy toad toast.

You're not aware you needed a toad?
You've never noticed me as I roam?
My work keeps pesty mosquitoes in check
Be glad I like to live at your home.

PROMISE FOR FEBRUARY

Groundhog day must come and go
Winter surrenders his blanket of snow
Icy winds don't continue to blow
The sun tries very hard to show.
Spring-like signs we yearn to know
Like daffodils about to glow.

The tulip with an upturned face
Will greet the gentle rain's embrace.
Tiny green leaves will begin to sprout
Old man winter will begin to pout
He'll go packing and he won't be missed
Our garden goddess deserves to be kissed.

A FRESH START

As I was returning from a solitary walk,
Under the leaves, I heard fairies talk.
"Look up", said one, "see the willow's hair,
It has turned to gold on the largest tree there."
That is the signal that winter has fled
That we can be sure spring is here instead.
We may smooth our wings wrinkled from sleep
Explore the forest glen and dance in the deep.
Let us go to seek the violet sweet,
But watch out for daffodil's stiff sharp feet.
If a soft, tender rain drifts from the sky
The crocus will appear in the wink of an eye
Lovely lilacs will provide fragrance fair
Sweet woodruff will sweeten the fresh, tender air.
Bell shaped lilies must throw off a leafy quilt
Song sparrows will sing of the nest they have built.
We might find the anemone near the woody pond
And search out the ferns tender new frond.
Let's tease awake the furry brown bear
And admire the baby foxes deep in their lair.
Hurry, gather your helpers for a busy flight
The gentle season has returned overnight."

THE ANNUAL MEETING

It was their annual meeting
They gathered near a star
The fairies of the garden
Flew in from fields afar.
They whispered to each other
Before the gavel fell
The secrets and remembrances
They could hardly wait to tell.
The business of the evening
To select the plantman's prize
Set the fairies to discussing
Who could ever be so wise?
Radiant and confident
Each arose to gently praise
Their friendly, favorite gardener
Whose flowers they helped to raise

After they finished voting
They whispered sweet good byes
Hugged and waved their fairy wands
To hide their teary eyes.
Fairies of the garden
Hate seeing the summer fade
Hate folding their fairy wings
Hate leaving the grassy glade.
Even fairies of the gardens
Must heed the season's plan
And hide away like flowers
Keeping safe in winter's span.

AS YOU LIKE IT

Snow flakes are never alike, they say
Because for some they are work
For some they are play.
Snow means fun for the young-hearted age,
For shovelers and plowers it means extra wage.
The thousands of patterns nature floats down on us
Sometimes tie up traffic for trains, cars and bus.
Those of us who have lost childlike fun in the snow
See drifts as a nuisance to shovel or blow.
Storms deliver a mighty cause of winter woe
Delaying a flight, broken ankles, or frozen toe.
Apologies to skiers we make, of course
And to those who can find a sure-footed horse.

PRAYER AT REST

Dear God, on my vacation
There was time for contemplation—
I saw your glory in the sunsets golden
Your majesty in the flight of the heron
Your humor in the diving ducklings
Your grandeur in the rainbow's arc
Your power in the crashing thunder
Your grace in elderly faces
Your love in mothers' embraces
Your thoughtful care of your kingdom
Your peace in the silence of the forest
Your goodness in this blessed nation
Your pride in your splendid creation.
I felt love of friends You gave me
I found support in those You placed near.
And I am grateful.

MY PORCH

Neighbors will climb the steps from the street
I welcome them all to my porch to meet

The pleasure of my porch I freely share
Of my comfortable place friends are aware.

Here these knotty panels, these irridescent panes
Comfort and conceal me as daylight wanes

Incandescent pictures in pink and purple ink
Reflect blushing leaves as sun tries to sink.

It's my own hiding place from vexing care
When morrow's thoughts I need to prepare

So join me for a visit or to dream or to read
The porch of my home will suit every need.

INTERNATIONAL HERB WEEK

We gather as herbers today to rejoice
We come to name the herb of our choice.

———

We celebrate HERB WEEK with a special meal
To let the world know about our herbal zeal.
We've found in herbs such varied delight
We've used these herbs for taste just right.
Herbs can be of use in many good ways
They're in kitchens and gardens every day.
We discover their pleasure anew each spring
We uncover more of the secrets herbs bring.
Raise up your voices, let us all sing
Hurrah for this week when the herb is the king.
Herbers are the first to find early green shoots
We know how to enjoy the leaves and the roots.
How to blend the powder of dried up remains
To make up herbal tea or a healthy tisane.
We're mindful of the history the herb has made.
We admire herb's goodness in life it played.
It's as timeless as thyme so let's give a cheer
It's the week of the year when herbs are most dear.

THE NATIONAL HERB GARDEN PLEA

Herbers, herbers, don't be contrary
How will our garden grow?
With silver coins, generous checks
And leafy green bills in a row.

Herbers, herbers, don't be contrary
Why must our garden grow?
It's there for all the world to view
It must be supported by each of you.

Herbers, herbers, don't be contrary
Where does our garden grow?
The National Herb Garden plot
In Washington D. C., the nation's spot.